The Little Black Box

I Got Out... Will YOU?

Tonya N. McGee Copyright© 2022

EMPOWER ME BOOKS, INC.
A Subsidiary of Empower Me Enterprises, Inc.

No part of this book may be reproduced, stored in a retrieval system, or transmitted in any form or by electronic, mechanical, photocopying, recording, scanning, or otherwise, without the publisher's prior written permission.

Scriptures marked KJV are taken from the KING JAMES VERSION (KJV): KING JAMES VERSION, public domain. They are used with permission.

ISBN: 978-1954418011
Printed in the United States of America

DEDICATION

- In Loving Memory of my mom, -
Lucinda C. McGee

We did it together through all my difficulties and everything we went through. My mom had always had my back, even when I did not know there was a back for her to have.

I thank God for her daily and everything she instilled in me as an adult woman.
Never give up; always take care of yourself and your children, and God will always see you through.

Mom told me that there was nothing on this earth and the one to come that she would not do for me. I will always and forever cherish every moment in this lifetime with her.

ACKNOWLEDGMENTS

There are too many people to acknowledge in such a limited space. God has placed so many people in my life that I cannot count them all. Even my enemies need to know I thank them for what I have been through and have overcome. But God!! I want to start by thanking my Pastors at One Love Christian Church. Pastor John and Co-Pastor Pauline Fitzpatrick taught me that Love could be honest if you allow it to be. But it must follow other components; respect and honor are necessary if you say you love someone. I am thankful for these two souls for standing in the gap when I could not stand for myself.

I acknowledge my children for keeping me on my toes. I wanted to live a life before them that was pleasing to God, and they made sure I did.

Destinee for always wanting to know why God is so good and what does it mean to live for him. Tony for asking just the right questions that led him to Jesus because he did not want to leave without me forever. Malcolm for making me mom and having to take care of him even when I did not know how to take care of myself. My children are the joy of my life, the reason I live and breathe. Thank you, guys, for understanding that mom must work because she loves you.

I dare not stop without acknowledging my Mother, Lucinda, my brothers Maurice and Jeris, their wives who are not only my sister-in-law but have grown to be my sisters, period Trina and Bonita. My Godmother Evelyn and my Godsisters and brothers, I love you all more than you could or would ever know.

I thank God for the great and powerful women he placed in my life. They do not know what an impact they have had on me, and I cannot begin to tell them how much they mean to me. Thank you, Minister Rhonda, Pastor Debra Cheek, Elder Rhonda; these women prayed for me, encouraged me, uplifted me, and were always a phone call away.

FOREWORD

BY Evelyn McGee

I want to thank God above for this young lady; she has indeed been a light in my life. I will honor her mom for allowing me to be her God mom!!!! I am so proud of you, Tonya Nichole McGee. You did just what the world said you could not do. You overcame every obstacle that the enemy threw in your path. Though it was hard to push through, Thank God you endured! I have known you all your life, and I have always known you would be somebody worth being close to. You are a good friend, a great sister in the Lord, and the best niece and goddaughter anyone could ask for.

I want to encourage you to never give up on your dreams. God has so much more in store for you. Allow him to use you so that he may get the glory out of your life. You have come this far by faith, leaning on the Lord. You have trusted in His word, and I can see he has never failed you yet. Everyone you will encounter, and those you have met will never be the same. There is something special in You. Continue to share yourself with the world. It only gets better from here. The winds may blow but stand steadfast on God's foundation before you. I am and have always been proud of you.

Evelyn McGee
Evangelist
New Vision Restoration Center
Peachtree Corners, Georgia

PREFACE

When I began to prepare this message that I will share through my Life's testimony, I began to feel overwhelmed; panic entered. I began to overthink, saying to myself, "Lord surely no one wants or needs to hear my story, people have been through much worse. Some are going through even worse now". God said to me, "It is not about what you went through. It is more about how you went through your things". I have never shared my contents outside of my religious group due to safety; I knew they would not judge me. They would walk along beside me. The more I tried to reason with God about how much I did not want to share this message and testimony, the more he pushed. So here we are!

This will be a short read, but I would like to tell you that loving yourself is a process! You have to love yourself even when it seems as though no one else does. This was hard for me when I was young, being told things like you're ugly fat nobody cares no one will believe you being physically abused emotionally abused you start to think those types of things when you're a little girl I hid in my little black box just like the enemy said no one would or did believe me and so like many of the things I went through where I was often told you better not tell what goes on in my house as a kid I took all of this back to my safe place where was my safe place you might ask my little black box.

    No one could hurt me there, so I thought. No one has a key here except me; only I had the address. Years later, I would come to understand how untrue that was. I was not the only one with a key there, and I was not safe. In that little black box, a few neighbors joined me. I do not even recall inviting them; however, hate joined me. Despair came to see me; depression showed up, and Self-pity walked right in. Fear came in and created a room and sometimes took over. Then with him came all his demonic friends.

Have you ever asked God to bless you or ever prayed for the increase? I used to sing about this in my darkness, recalling it now precisely what I was asking God to enlarge? I have gotten so good at dressing the part; I looked okay. I even talked okay, but I was not okay. I knew the Lord, and I knew that he loved me. I knew that he loved me so much that I would ask him to send someone to see about me, and someone would come. However, they could not stay long because they could not understand or fathom the level of brokenness I was in. They would stay for a while and then leave me to myself with my box full of roommates.

I often prayed, "Lord, I need someone to lead me out of this place. I know you hear me, God, and I know that people have come in the past, but no one wanted to pull me out of here.

They knocked, they visited, and then they left."

This book is for that someone who is reaching out. This book is for the person you know who may be reaching out to you, and check on that person if they are. Make sure they are doing well. Check on the ones that look the part; the ones that are dressed the part; the ones with the big smiles, who always seem like they are doing good. Check on the ones with the children that are doing good and not giving them trouble; the one with an excellent job and the one with the good husband, friend, etc. Those are the people that are most often stuck inside their little black box. These are the ones who need to know how to love themselves enough to walk out of the dark place and not return. These are the friends, family members, church attendants, and co-workers who need to be encouraged with more than words; they do not even need your things. Let me just tell you that depressed people do not want to be depressed; people who are suicidal do not want to die. People that need help do not always look like they need help. They look powerful, and they get tired. The world forces them to be extraordinarily strong.

To those of you who are going through anything that could lead to depression, low Self-esteem, self-loathing, and much more, I want you to start loving yourself now. I will share my stories with you to encourage you, to let you know that it is okay, but I want you to tell yourself daily that you *ARE* loved! Go on that coffee date with a friend. Schedule weekly dates to meet up with a sister or join a gym class even when not feeling like it. Finding ways to support others is an impressive mood booster. Being around people that love you will help you feel less depressed, and when it is easier to retreat into that little black box, turn your key in and love yourself enough to leave. I promise you are worth it, not only to yourself but first to God.

CONTENTS

DEDICATION
ACKNOWLEDGMENTS
FOREWORD
PREFACE

Section I   - Overcoming Childhood Trauma 26
Section II - Overcoming Marital Trauma 57
Section III - Overcoming Church Hurt Trauma 79

Affirmations - Reminders that Affirm God's Love for YOU! 99

BOOK REVIEWS 108
ABOUT THE AUTHOR 111

The LITTLE black BOX

SECTION I

Overcoming Childhood Trauma

I Got Out... Will YOU

Section I – Introduction
Overcoming Childhood Trauma

Growing up as we all know it, children sometimes have lots of challenges, whether family, friends, school or life itself. As for me, I thought I had the worst childhood ever. Some people may think that that was not accurate, and I am sure some grew up with more problems than I could ever have. But mine was the worst for me, and the same would be for them; theirs were the worst. I never thought that my mother did not love my brothers and me; however, I felt we came at a terrible time in her life. She wanted to be free, and it was hard to do that with three children.

At some point in my life, I had to be

some kind of misfit. I tried so hard to impress so many people in my family. I wanted them to love me like they love everyone else. That did not work for me. So here goes my downward roll into my little black box. A box that I came to own that no one could take me out of. I controlled it; I controlled who came in and who went out. Even if I never allowed anyone in, I was still in control. It was my way of saying if you do not care about me, I will hide away, never to be seen again.

My little black box was my safety net; at least I thought I was safe there. I realized that I was not safe there, but I was also alone. I did not allow anyone in or out. I was also stuck in a hole where I had created it all myself. "I am sure someone will come looking for me one day. I am sure they will miss me and know that I need them to recuse me from myself." These were my inner thoughts and personal conversation, but no one came, no one looked for me, no one cared enough to love me.

What was it about me that I was so unlovable? Why did everyone I tried to impress ignore me, push me aside, and forget that I belonged? Now, of course, they would say no, we did not do that. But every time they left me to be belittled at someone else's hands, they had pushed me aside. Whenever they overlooked me when I was trying so hard, I felt ignored. Every time they made me feel invisible; so, back to my safety net, back to my prison, the one I created for myself because of them.

I will survive this trauma; I will someday find a way to break away and throw the keys to this box into the sea of forgiveness o remember it no more. One day, right??

CHAPTER 1

Shut the Hell up!!! Those were common words to me as a kid. I used to think that curse words were another language I heard so much. Life for me as a child was not the best in my perspective; of course, others would think I had the best of the best. Of course, we looked good on the outside, but the house on the inside was a wreck. The foundation was firm, but if one were to knock on it too hard, we could all very well die inside. People often told me, "Girl, you got it made. Your parents take great care of you. Your clothes are always clean, and your hair is always done. You are a big girl. I know you are not going without any meals," they would say. But no one knew what was happening in my world behind closed doors when no one was watching.

It was very easy to be outside looking in when you lived in a house with only one window. Living my life was, to me, very taxing. I had my mom, two brothers, and yes, my stepfather. People said, "Girl, any man that would marry a girl with two children was a good man. But was he? My mother had my other little brother and me before she got married, and after she was married, five years later, she had my baby brother. I love my brothers to life; there is nothing I would not do for them, take for them, or protect them from. I often had to be the one to protect them from a lot at the hands of my stepfather. But even then, I found myself alone.

I never felt like he liked me or even tried to like me. Of course, he was the best when other family members were around, and no one knew the damage he was creating when we were alone behind locked doors. We were told often, you better not ever say to no one what goes on in my house. Of course, we were very obedient; we did not say to a soul. So I never felt loved by anyone because of this. I was never alone to talk to anyone about how I felt and what I was going through as a child.

When I was very young, I used to say, "Lord, please help me because one day this man is going to kill me and no one will ever notice. No one will look for me; no one will miss me, cry over me or fight for my justice in the matter." When I was around ten years old, things became worse for me. I would get in trouble for everything. I could not ask for anything, and that included food. He used to say, "You don't need nothing to eat; you're big enough." But doesn't everyone have to eat to live? Many things happened in my life, but one thing that stuck out to me was among the many things that happened around age 12. It was a life-changer for me, even as young as I was. I knew then that I had to find a way to escape. I knew that I had to do it fast or I would not last.

CHAPTER 2

This day I was sitting on my front porch in lawn chairs that my mom had put out there. She likes to have chairs on the porch, so when she came home on some days, she would sit outside and talk to our neighbor - just to sit and smoke. This was her way of unwinding after working two jobs. See, my stepfather did not work, and like most Black women, she did what she had to do to make sure we had clothes, shelter, and food. I know sometimes it was hard for her, and the ends did not meet all the time. Remembering those times made me part of the woman I have become today. I knew that I would always make sure my children had, and they knew that I loved them unconditionally no matter what.

So, on the porch where I was sitting this summer afternoon, there were about five chairs out there; I was already sitting in one, so that made four of the free. One of my brothers was playing ball in the yard, and my baby brother was in the house taking a nap.

While sitting, the door opened, and it was my baby brother, "can I come outside," He asked me. I told him, "Sure, but you have to go and put your shoes on." I was happy he was up from his nap; I love him dearly. He was like a doll to me. I could hold him, dress him, and so on. My brother kept messing with the door because he did not want to put on shoes, and I was already warned that if I came back into the house, I could not come back out. Therefore, I did not want to go in because that would be trouble. I told him to stop messing with the door and get his shoes.

Of course, my stepfather was in the house, and he heard us and thought we were playing with the door. It appears that man always looked for opportunities to belittle me, call me names, and beat on me. Yes, I was always bruised somewhere on my body. We covered it up nicely. They went as far as being burned with hot pasta to having picture frames dropped on your head and blood running down my face bruised. Who could I tell? Who would even believe me? I was invisible to my outside family. They did not see me as they saw the other children in the family. I did not, for the life of me, understand that. I could not tell my mom because I did not think she ever believed what I was saying, so what did I do? I suffered in silence, in pain, and sometimes most of the time, wishing I were dead. At least then, I would have an end to all the things he was putting me through as a child. No child should have to endure these things.

This day was a biggy; my brother would not stop messing with the door because we wanted to come outside without shoes, and mom did not allow us outside without shoes on. She did not want us to trample mud and dirt back in the house from our bare feet. I would not let him out because he did not have on shoes. After about five or ten minutes or so of me going back and forth with my brother, he busted out the door. Before I could even speak, my stepfather had picked up the chair I was sitting in and threw it to the ground with me still in it. I yelled stop, and then he threw the other chairs from the porch at me, hitting me everywhere on my body. Blood was going all over the place as I cried and screamed, please STOP; someone helps me! I cried to the top of my lungs. No one was home to recuse me; mom was at work, my aunt that lived across the street was at work. I was then at the mercy of my neighbors. By the grace of God, someone called the police. When I heard the sirens, I was so happy that this pain would be over soon. The whole time he threw chairs at me, he cursed me and said he wished that I were not here; well, so did I!

I asked God, Why Me, God? What did I do? Why is my mom not here to help me? I have no one. This cannot be real life; no one goes through being abused, physically, mentally, and emotionally all simultaneously. Of course, only me.

The police called an ambulance, and

they came and checked me over bandaged me up. I had cuts and bruises on my head, the back of my legs, and my back. They were so shocked and concerned that I was so afraid to leave with them because I knew what I was told about talking to anyone about anything that went on in my mom's house. The call must have gone out over the police scanner because my mom was called, and my birth father was called, of course, and that is a different story. The police took my stepfather away, and the neighbor came over with my brothers and me until my mom arrived. Thank you, Jesus. I am finally free! I am safe!! No more abuse, YES!

My mom drove up, and I cried and called out to her. "Mom, mom!" I began to tell her what had happened. She watched the police drive away with him in the car.

Come on in this house; she said to me in a voice not so pleasant, did I do something wrong. Am I in trouble for what he had done to me? I did not talk to anyone; I did not tell anyone what was happening in the house. It was me that was hurt and beaten. So why is she mad at me? I did not understand then, and sometimes It takes the grace of God for me to understand even now. When I got in the house, she yelled at me to take a bath and go to bed because I had school tomorrow; now you know we have to cover up these bruises. I did not care because I just knew my life would change. But was it? The night was long, but it was so peaceful this was the first time in a long time. I could sleep and not worry about what would happen to me. I got up on my own and began to get ready for school; I was so happy that I did not even care about the bruises anymore; I just knew I would not have to endure pain like this ever again, not from home and not from him. At least, that is what I thought. The charges were dropped, and when I got home from school, who was there? Yes, he was. My nightmare had just begun. Why did she drop the charges? Lord, I do not understand. Does she not love me? Did I not matter? Was I not important? Was it because I was fat? Am I all the things he said I was? When he said you are ugly and nobody cares and that I was stupid etc., was it true?

It did not matter if I called my daddy or not because he did nothing to help me. I will never be anything because he ran this house, is what I was told. My only thought was, why me? He silenced me for the rest of my childhood. I went through so much more during the time that I climbed into my little black box; I was simply there. I turned sixteen, and I knew it was time to go. I could not take any more of what was happening to me behind these closed doors. I did not want to be seen anymore. I was scorned for life. And now I was scared for my life. I figured I would be what he and others thought about me. I am an outcast. I could not show love because I did not know love.

CHAPTER 3

Did this affect me as a child? Why yes, I do believe it did. It affected me as a child, but it also affected me as an adult. There were so many things I am not allotted time to tell you about that went on in the childhood that impacted me and how I journeyed through life. I was afraid to make friends; I was scared to talk to people because I felt as though I was stupid and that my words did not matter. I had become a shy person that everyone saw during such a late age in my life. I felt as though no one would or could accept me for who I was because of all the things placed in my spirit. No one got me. So, if my family did not love and appreciate me, why should strangers? The things send me farther into depression than ever before. But of course, I did not know what depression was. However, I did understand that I was not happy. I was not okay by any means.

The things I endured as a child made me a loner. I walked around as if I was invisible. I thought to myself, if no one could see me, I would be fine. I could make it. The more abuse I went through, the deeper I got into my little black box. The farther I packed myself away from the world. I began even to hate myself. I did not believe I was normal anymore because ordinary people did not have things like what I had been through happen to them. Someone loves everyone. No matter how much I excelled in school, I never felt like I mattered. I thought like a child, and this is how it is supposed to take all the abuse from whoever and be quiet. I was forced to grow up and grow up fast. While in my box, I managed to talk myself into doing good in school to escape this life and what it was throwing at me. I had no one and no life, no friends. Even as an adult, I had no one, no energy, and no friends. I never heard the words I love you; I never had hugs and kisses or attention, for that matter. I did know that when I got out, I hoped I would not be this way when I get good and grown. I did not want to be the shy one. I did not want to be the one that never talked and never took a risk. It was hard for me to overcome. I did not go places; I even stopped asking people if I could go places with them. I felt like if they did not want me around, I did not want to be around them.

I got a part-time job and buried

myself in my feelings. So as an adult, nothing changed. I did not think I was worthy of anything. I did not deserve to be loved; that is what I was told all my childhood, so it must ring true. So, I thought. I married the first man that asked me, and I knew he loved me, but I did not know how to love him. I remember when I was younger; I told myself that when I have children of my own, I will love them to pieces. I am going to show them every day how much I love them. I will hug them, kiss them and give them attention. I will tell them how much they mean to me, and I will never allow anyone to hurt them. I was going to try and shelter them from this wicked world. I was always on my guard about my children, and I would always be.

My adult life was very much affected by my childhood. I discovered that I was withdrawn and did not like being in crowds. I felt that people would see what everyone else saw of me, and that was nothing. I did not talk much, and I would never take risks. I was fearful and had anxiety about everything. I never thought I could or would be anything in life. I felt that my childhood had ruined my chance of me ever being productive in this world. That is what the enemy wanted me to believe. He wanted me to fear, not trust, and hate myself as I thought others did.

I had to learn that it was all a trick of the enemy, which is not what God had for me. God's intentions for me were pure and rich. My life meant something to him even when I was formed in my mother's womb. God had a purpose for me. He knew that I would have to go through trials, and he was preparing me to make a breakthrough.

He knew that he would get the glory out of my life, and someday I would be able to share my story fully with someone going through it, and they would be set free. I was no longer that little girl anymore; I was royalty bought with a price. I belong to a priesthood of kings and queens. I am the child of the most high God. It took me a long time to get this, but he was more than the whole world against me as long as God was for me. So even when the devil says you are not loved, know that you are loved when he thinks you will never be anything know that you are already something and somebody. God loved me even when I did not love myself. He STILL loves me, and he loves you too!

CHAPTER 4

The spirits that I found attached to me during these times were powerful, and when you fed them, they became stronger. I fed them daily, so they overtook me and my mental abilities. I no longer belonged to myself but to the things that controlled me.

FEAR The spirit of fear had encapsulated me the most. It had me whipped; it talked to me every day, every hour, and every min of my life. It had me believing things that I know now could never be true. I had conversations with him, Fear that is, all the time. People laughed at me, and I believed darkness was my friend. PITY is what fear showed me all the time. I had compassion for myself, and I did not believe I could be anything, and pity was there to egg me on. I was not worthy of anyone's affection, and pity constantly whispered this to me. I was not deserving of even God's love, not to mention the love from my family.

Pity took me places in my mind that I could not recover from or I thought I could recover from. I needed help from drowning in this darkness, and fear and pity kept me bound. I did not know how to ask for help, and this demon grew from this daily. It grew with every tear I shredded, and my little black box got darker and darker. I had no hope. I began to HATE. HATE is where fear and pity took me; I hated myself, so I understood why others could and did hate me. I did not like what I saw in the mirror, so I understood why others did not like what they saw when they saw me. There is no way anyone could have a love for a worthless person like myself. I hated to get up in the mornings.

When I did get up, I ate as much as I could because I was afraid I would not have enough to eat. "What was the purpose of being here in the world if you are not loved or needed;" so I thought. *These demons laughed at me daily,* and *yet they became my friends.* They were the only ones that made sense because I had heard this all my life. Sometimes I did not know who had me the tightest; fear, pity, or hate. They all go hand in hand, and one cannot live without the other.

If I was going to get rid of one, I had to get rid of them all at the same time, all together. I understood that these things were from Satan himself, and they came to torment me. They were very skillful and diligent, and they were not easy to get rid of; they had been with me all my life. Why would they want to leave now? I had fed them and nurtured them as though they were all I had in this world, But God!!

As I came to know, you must understand that God is always in control, that he would never leave you, nor will he forsake you. I had to learn that even in my valley, God was there. He told me yes though I walk through the valley of the shadow of death, I should fear no evil for though art with me!!! So even in my valley, God was and is with me. He was not standing on the other side; he walked me through. He held my hand and carried me even when I could not bring myself. When I could not pray for myself, Jesus stood in intercession and prayed for me. When I fell, God was there to pick me up, dust me off, and let me know that it was okay and that he had me. He would say, "I love you; I have affection towards you."

God was there to help me forgive my stepfather; he showed me what real love was. He reminded me that if I were in him, and he was in me, I would have a genuine agape love for everyone. He showed me how to love my enemies and those who despitefully used me. Was it hard to forgive? No. I thought it would be, and I even cried when I had to go back and face the demon that bound me for so many years of my life. But when I did go back, all I felt was peace and peace that passed all understanding. A peace that no man can give you a peace that if it were not for Jesus, I would not have.

Forgiveness is vital when you want to break chains in your life. Set the people who did you wrong free by forgiving them; you intern will be set free. You can then walk out of that little black box the same way I walked out of the little black box that had me in bondage for so many years. Then you, too, can throw away the keys. Take back what the enemy thinks he took from you and allow God to heal your heart. One of my old pastors used to say, "it is not a hard thing. It is a heart thing."

Prayer to Overcome Childhood Trauma

Lord, thank you for coming to my rescue, and just like you did it for me, God, I know you can and will do it for them. I speak peace to every person reading this and have had to endure any of the pain I have been through. Come Lord and establish your dominion of peace in God. I know you have not given the spirit of fear, but of love power and sound mind and God, I claim that for them today. God, I pray and ask that you be a sponge and draw from them every pain, trauma, fear, shock, and shame that the enemy has placed on them and in their minds. God, we come against any ruling powers of darkness that were sent to impede the mature walk of Christ in your son and daughters. We call out all spirits connected, rooted, and ruling in the areas of depression, addiction, manipulation, stress, loneliness, and hopelessness. Pour your grace on them, God and your mercy restore them to a state of completeness to include your fruit of the spirit in Jesus' name, amen.

The LITTLE black BOX

SECTION II

Overcoming Marital Trauma

I Got Out...
Will YOU

Section II – Introduction
Overcoming Marital Trauma

Being in love is sometimes a difficult thing. I found myself constantly wondering in the back of my mind if the person I placed all this confidence in was even worth my love. One can discover themself having crazy feelings about minor simplistic things. It is often all in your head, and the very thing you are worried about only exists in your mind. What does it mean to be in love? Is it that feeling you get when you are in high school, or even that far is it the feeling when you get your first crush? I had to look it up to get a good meaning of what being in love meant. Even in my reading, I found it hard to tell if you just love someone or are really in love with them, especially if this is a new thing for you. See, I never really encountered the feeling that someone was or has ever been in love with me.

I understand that I have a choice whether I love someone or not but being in love with them is a whole other ball game. Being in love happens without you evening knowing what is going on; it is not a choice. Suppose it was who would choose to be in love with the chance that it may hurt in the end. It is not something you can simply walk away from, that is for sure. It stays with you no matter where you try to hide. I can use the example of how God loves us. No matter where we go, what we do well or bad, he still loves us. He loves us without restrictions. He always loves us and promises never to leave us or forsake us. God puts us first even when we do not put ourselves self-first.

CHAPTER 5

Where is he; I thought to myself? It is well into the wee hours of the night, and everyone in my house is sleeping, everyone but me and, of course, him. Because he is not here and here, I am like the fool I was, up waiting for him. God knew that my Spouse at that time was not coming home and that I would have to go out looking for him again. I prayed that things were okay, but when he was out, things were never OK. How could it be when he was putting that poison in his body repeatedly? What could I do but pray while I waited and prayed while I looked?

"Lord, show me where to go; where he is?" It has been three days now, and I am worried. I put on my shoes and coat because it is cold outside, grab my keys and purse, and head for the door. I was trying not to wake anyone up in the house because I did not want to say where I was going and why. After getting into the car, I asked the Lord again, "please show the path to take and which road to go on so I can help somehow. He is my husband, and this hurts." I started the car and began to drive. It was 3 am, and what came to my mind was the idea that the only people out were drug users, dealers, and the homeless.

I drove down street after street, praying and looking. After about an hour of driving, I came upon his van parked outside this old-looking house. Many other cars were there, but I could and would recognize his van anywhere. When I saw His van, I knew I would have to go into that house and get him out of that. I knew that he was not going to just come out on his own, and if he did, it would be the following day.

I have had so many times when I would try to wait for my ex-husband out to see if he would leave when I saw the car or van, but I learned the hard way that it would not happen. I have been drugged down the street a time or two trying to get him to leave a place and come home with me. I was always trying to save him from himself. God, I pray to help me help him. Help me, God, to bring him home. I got myself together, parked the car, and started to get out of the vehicle. I left everything in the car, but my keys and I walked up to the house's front door, and I knocked, and I knocked unto it turned into banging.

Finally, a Black man answered the door, and when he looked up at me, it was as though he had seen a ghost. I looked at him, and when he said, "Who was it, and what did I want?" I told him I wanted the man that was driving that van. I told him his name, and the Black man moved aside and showed me the room's door where he was. They were all coughing and talking in that room, yelling and fussing at each other, and the door was locked so no one could get in. The man knocked on the door, called his name, and told him he had to come out because some people wanted to see him. When he said that I knew I was alone, I did not correct the man because I wanted him out of there. He knocked again, and a woman's voice came and said, "get away from the door," but the man repeated himself and said, "send him out." "He has to go so these people can leave my house." I knew then that God was with me. I felt a boldness that I had never felt before, and I called his name and said, come out and let's go.

The door opened, and they pushed him out of the room. The man told him, "Bro, you got to get out of here," he was all sweaty and red-eyed, smelling awful, looking amusing like the colloquium goes, "he looked like who did it and why." I knew he was not in his right mind, and I knew he could not see what that man saw. The man asked me if I would please take my friend and leave; I grabbed him by the hand and pulled him out of the house onto the street where his van was parked. He had cleaned out his bank account in three days. He had not been to work in three days, so of course, he had lost that job and shoplifting, so now he has a charge to deal with all because he wanted to get high. I started to cry, I was confused, and I was cold. So, I told him he had to go with me now, or it was never. I explained to him that this was hurting not only him but his family to no end and that he was putting us in a place that made it hard to come back from. Money wasted, time lost, it was a never-ending story.

I yelled and yelled and begged him to come home. Why did I have to beg a man that supposed to love his children and me to go home? "Why did I have to beg a man that was supposed to be the head of my house to come home"? I was supposed to be the helpmeet, and here I am, taking care of him instead of him taking care of me. I knew the Lord was with me because I felt his presence, and it was stronger than I had ever felt before. I pulled that big man to my car and made him get in, and it felt as if it was done with ease. I prayed for deliverance for him and me. He got in the car and left his van there at that house. I started the car and began to drive home. I cried all the way home. Of course, he talked and made empty promises never to do this again. I did what any wife would do.

I forgave him again, just like I did when he stole my wedding rings, and when he stole all the food out of the house, and when he disappeared for two months. I always forgave him and took him back, hoping things would change that he would someday see the hurt he was causing and change his ways. Why was everything I did in vain; why were things not changing? Why is this still going on and on? *Am I helping him, or am I hurting me?* I had to learn to depend solely on God. I knew that I could not save him no matter what I did.

God was the giver of salvation, and no matter what I said or did, it was only between him and God. So many times, he has hurt the family and me with his drug problem. I stayed because I loved him, not wanting the enemy to have what God had chosen as significant. You would have thought that when he pulled me down the road while driving the car and me holding on to the door, I would have known then it was all about his drugs, but I did; I still stayed. Seeing him jump out of windows because he wanted to get high and I would move from in front of the door, I should have known the enemy had control, and there was nothing I could do but pray. Sometimes I did not know how to feel. I thought, "if I could just be a better wife," things would be different, but was it me? How would I pull myself away from this toxic way of life? I allowed the enemy to put me back in that bondage box again, this time because of love. This love was one-sided.

I was in just as much bondage as my now ex-husband. The same drugs, the same demon behind the drug that had him bound, had me. He knew if he could control my husband, that same demon knew he could also hold me. He wanted to destroy me just as fast. At the time, he had been doing a great job at it.

He wanted me to believe that God was not who he said he was in my life. He was not a healer and deliverer. The enemy wanted me to think that God was a liar. He wanted me to believe that when God said he loves me, he did not mean it or that God would not allow these things to happen. I am his servant, faithful, and love God, and here I was, spiraling down a dark black hole and going through a tunnel with no end. I could not see the light at the end. The devil had me in a tight clutch more than I thought he did. I had to find a way to stop and see that he was pulling my heart string just as hard as he was pulling my husband.

I had to come face to face with the fact that this was reality, and I had to learn how to survive. I lived in a fantasy world, and things would never get better until I took my hands off it and allowed God to be God in this situation. My husband had to decide to get better for himself; it was not a magical thing, and it would not disappear overnight. Addictions are rooted or derived from spirits that attack one's character personality traits and can attack or evolve based on circumstance. And yes,

I know it can happen to anyone. I had been fighting the fight to no avail, and the devil thought he had bought me to my knees. He thought I was broken without repair. He thought he had me just where he wanted me, and his job was done.

    I remembered the story in the bible when Jesus delivered the man with the unclean spirits as he came out of the tomb; of course, demons possessed that man, but what I see is depressed, lonely, departed a person with no hope they are all demons. Buried in a hole, a dark place, and a box that was running out of room, the more I thought about the demons-possessed man, the more It gave me hope, knowing that I had all the help I needed right here in my box. Somehow, I figured out how to mask my pain behind the shadow of a smile and dedicate my life to helping people I was doing the most when I felt the worst. And I was still suffering in silence. I could not let go; I had just gotten good at hiding in the corners in the shadows. I was good at locking myself away; I was a closet coward.

CHAPTER 6

The spirits I saw daily were depression, addiction, manipulation, stress, loneliness, and hopelessness. These demons will leave you feeling like your purpose means nothing. They will have you feeling like you mean nothing. I had to come to my senses and say that God is still a keeper of his word no matter what I was going through or what I had been through. I had to bring myself back to the understanding that I could depend on the word of God in any storm. God promised to deliver me, and he is not slack on his promises. I know that trials will come, but God will give me what I need to get through them. He will attain me. I have the victory in Christ Jesus. He is my light. He is my salvation and should have no worries.

The Apostle Peter said, do not be surprised at fiery trials that we go through as though it was strange, but be glad for everything we go through because it brings you closer to Christ. God gave me strength for that day and the next day and the days to come. Because he promised me he would. He gave me the sun when I needed it and rain when my life felt empty and dry. And though I had sorrow, there was joy waiting for me. There was often so much pain to bear, but God gave me peace to abound. I had to go back to my old bible teaches and remind myself how God delivered the three men from the fiery furnace. I know God can and will provide me with these flames. These were attacks from the evil one not only for my addictive husband but also for me. I had to learn to spend more time with God in prayer; that is where my power would come from. He loves me, and I had to learn it for myself. God was working on my behalf even when I was running up and down the streets in the late-night hours looking for the man supposed to take care of my children and me. When I was about to lock the doors on my box, never to come out again, God's truth immense I got great peace and comfort because I now know and understand the scripture; I can do all things through Christ that strengthens me.

Call on God because when we call on him, he goes to work angels are sent on our behalf to work in our favor. We might not understand it, but it is his perfect will and way. It will never lead you in the wrong direction; let go of what you are holding on to. I had to allow God to help me take control of my situation. Is my husband free? No, because he must let God do the work. Is he still addicted; yes, he is, but I am not. I am free from that bondage of pain; I will no longer allow the enemy to pull my heartstring again. God has again walked me through my dark place over to the other side. When I thought I would be alone, he reminded me you are never alone. When I thought I would make it with three children, he reminded me that he was my provider. When I thought I would lose my mind, God showed up and allowed me to see that he is the mind regulator!!

God will see your needs and meet them even when you are in your little black box. I prayed and prayed for wisdom, but I could never obtain it until I listened to wisdom. I was an enabler, and I hurt my husband, but I was also killing myself slowly. I had to realize that this was not love. When I learned to love him, I let him go to allow God to work in my favor on his behalf. I had to rebuild my family. I must rebuild my home to allow peace to shine where there had formerly been none. I could only do that by letting God's glory shine. I found my way out; I found peace in the valley again, and I was never alone. Jesus was always there; he told me, and I now believe him.

Prayer to Overcome Marital Trauma

God, Fill me with your Spirit and help me rid my heart of all the anger and hurt I have towards (*Insert the name of your spouse or ex-spouse*). Surround me, God, with your comfort, strength, and wisdom. Thank you, God, for pouring your love on me and never leaving me or forsaking me when I needed you the most. Thank you for allowing me to love again in Jesus' name, amen.

The LITTLE black BOX

SECTION III

Overcoming Church Hurt Trauma

I Got Out... Will YOU

Section III – Introduction
Overcoming Church Hurt Trauma

Church Hurt is something I am sure so many people go through. Some people handle church hurt. They continue to go to the church because of family tides, community, and some even because of status in the church, whether they are a minister, a teacher, an usher choir director, etc. At any rate, they decide to stay and continue in the abuse. Then there are the ones who decide they are not going to take the mental abuse, the embarrassment, the craziness that is going on, pack their things, and leave. Whichever way you and or others decide to go, do so with good intentions. Never leave a place without resolving the problem between you and

God because the problem goes with you when you leave. You may think, "Well, I have done a good deed," but the enemy is waiting on you at your next place, and then it becomes like a revolving door.

You do not want to be in and out of every church you go to and join. Make sure to speak to the ministry leaders and bring them into the knowledge of what is going on. This should be done long before you ever desire to leave; to ensure you are not emotional and that you are hearing God. Most of the time, these are things that can be resolved, and life can continue for all in peace and love. We must remember that church hurt will destroy the believer; it will mess up the mind of the saints, disappoint you, and discourage the saints of God. God is love, and love should always abide in the church from all that proclaim to be believers.

CHAPTER 7

Going to church for me as a child was an exciting time. It was easy to get up and go to church and not worry about what was going on with the people leaders or anything else. I was a kid. My grandmother would take me to church every Sunday, and I was ready. When to call came into my mom, "get my gal ready, I will be there to pick her up," was music to my ears. I loved the church and everything that went on in the church, from the singing to the shouting and the jumping around from the people, even the hoop and hollow of the preacher. Why did I love those things as a child? Well, because I was a child and while I was a child, I spoke as a child, and I thought as a child? I did not understand what it means to believe to be a Christian to be a saint of God. I knew I needed to be in church every Sunday because it was the right thing to do. It was how I thought and believed the church was supposed to go.

I did not have a real relationship with Christ. I also went because I loved being with my grandmother. Church to me in my younger years was where God lived. It was a place of peace where people got healed, where everyone loved everyone, and everyone was happy. Nothing in this building while there was supposed to hurt anyone. Nothing in this space was supposed to damage your sight of what you thought or felt about God. In this building, it was only supposed to be love, nothing more and nothing less. The love they told me covers a multitude of sins. So, when I was in this place and did not feel the love, I knew then that this was not a church where God lives. This is not where I belong, and I must move on. I could not nor would I leave the body of Christ, but my membership must move. I knew that deliverance was among the saints along everything else I needed was there with the true believers. I could get over and should get over the lack of love in the same place.

My grandmother passed away, which left me with no way to ever get to church. Mom would send me to random services such as vacation bible school youth services, which were all during the summer, but it was never like being in the presence of God. See though I was young, I could feel the difference when I was where truth abides. While growing up there, I saw so many things going on in the building that made me think why I am even attending church with all these shenanigans going on.

I saw pastors in clubs and then in the pulling pit preaching to me on Sundays, and yes, I saw them drinking and so forth, and I know I am not judge or jury; in any case, I was taught we had to be different we had to hold up a different standard than what was going on in the world. The bibles tell me that Jesus said to be holy for I am holy, so when I saw ministers and pastors, etc., and I know they are mere men, I did not expect to see them doing what I was doing at that time in my life. Of course, I know I was not supposed to be there, but I do not believe they should have been either. I saw deacons with women other than their own wives, people taken from the church, and many more things that were just not right in the sight of God or man. So, at 17, I stopped going to church.

CHAPTER 8

I did not feel that there was anything I could learn at that church. Everything I wanted to do, or I thought I wanted to do; I could do it without being a local assembly member.

One thing that did stick in my heart was that I loved to sing the gospels of Christ, so while I was in college, I joined the college gospel choir. I sang all I wanted to shoot. I knew these people were not right with God, and we're not pretending to be. They, just like me, had the gift to sing and decided to use it for God. All while still doing what we wanted to do. Even though I stopped going to church while in college, I knew I was missing something; I knew there was something in my life that I needed, and unbelievably it was church. The man I was dating and I decided we were going back to church precisely what we did.

It was great; I finally got what I was missing Jesus!! My heart was filled, and I had joy unspeakable joy. I gave my life to Christ, and I was a different person. Though I did not know everything I needed to see, I knew that Jesus loved me, and I loved him. I made church my life. When the doors of the church opened, I was in the building. So much so that when I got married, my husband was not so happy about me always being in church. I could not explain to him the feeling that Church allowed me to have. I knew it was a privilege to be able to serve the one and true living God. He stopped going to this church and said he would never attend again because he did not like its control over his family.

My pastor was a woman, and of course, I did not and could not see what my husband noticed when it came to controlling and manipulative behaviors. He would remember everything I used to tell him about the alcoholism, substance abuse, domestic violence, greediness, and sexual immorality that went on in my church when I was young. Though I could not see it, then he saw it. See, the pulpit was still silent regarding issues of sin and immoral behavior. There I was alone in church without my family, but I told the Lord that I live and for him, I die. I began to grow in the church leading platform, and I wanted to venture out and meet other young people like myself who loved the Lord. I found some friends I worked with, and they invited me to visit their church.

I knew that my pastor was not happy about us visiting other churches, so I just asked them to be obedient to the office that she walked in. Even though she did not want me to go, I went anyway, and Oh God, my eyes opened!! I learned things that the word of God said that we were never told about. I knew that most of the things we do in the church are manmade and that God only requires you to live Holy. I learned that since Jesus died for us, God has grace and mercy on us in the New Testament. This does not mean that we do not have to honor the Old-Testament; it simply means that God grants us grace now based on the intercessions made by Jesus and that he has fulfilled the law.

I could not believe all the things I had learned improperly that were not a part of the word of God. At that moment, when I visited this church, I knew this was where I needed to be and where God wanted me. God wants us to grow in him, and I was not growing where I was. I was finally on fire for the Lord and could not wait to continue spending the rest of my life serving him. The Holy Spirit was working in my life and on my behalf. And I was so excited about it.

My last Sunday at church was the worst. I did my hair and got dressed, and went in. When I got there, I could feel the shift in the air, and I knew it would be a war in the spirit that day. The pastor was on me like white on rice, as they say. I remember telling her that I had received the Gift of the Holy Ghost, and while in the pulpit, she said to us that nobody gets the holy spirit until she said they got it and that she had not confirmed it; therefore, we were liars and going to hell.

She talked about my hair, saying watch their dogs go around with the new hair. Instead of putting their money in the church, they give it to the hairstylist and how that was not of God. She did everything that morning but called my name. Of course, I cried through all the services because I knew this was my clue that it was time for me to move on. However, I still waited and did not listen to the voice of the Lord. Two weeks passed, and we were having a revival, and I so wanted to go, and I knew I did not have a way there, so I called my pastor and asked if I could ride with her; we did not have a large church, so we could always call and ask for car rides with others as needed. That is what we are called to do anyway, so I thought. Therefore, I asked the pastor if I could ride with her to church, and her response to me was, I do not ride members in my car; they ride me, and she was not picking me up and that I should find another way. I was crushed; what on earth did I do to deserve this from my pastor. I was hurt.

I called one of the ministers, and I told them that I would not be attending the church that night. I told them why and they said that I had to be there, and they would come and get me, did and we went. When I tell you, God whooped me from that night from that pulpit. God told me that I should have left when he told me to. Now, I had to endure the pain of not obeying him.

CHAPTER 9

God showed me himself through that speaker that night, and I knew this was my last night in that assembly. And the other members did as well. See, I learned that God wants us to respond to church hurt when it happens, and he gives us the tools to respond. I know what I know, and it worked for me, and I am sure it will work for you. First, always pray, remember when you get hurt in the church, that sometimes-church people are not good at loving on the people of God.

When we are hurt, always go to the source of love, and that is God himself. Cast all your cares on God, for he loves you. Remember, he will never hurt or abandon us. You are spending your time resting in his love so that you can be restored. Then it is okay to confront your offender. The bible tells us if your brother or sister offends, you tell them. If they do not listen, then take a witness. These problems can be resolved most of the time if you talk to the person who hurt you. This is not always an easy thing to do, but it is necessary.

You must understand that this put me in place in my life where I found it hard to trust women pastors again, and that experience placed me in a dark place, a little black box, where I remained for a long time. I withdrew every time I had to be in the presence of a woman preaching, and sometimes, I avoided going to hear them all together. It was hard to forgive, but I knew that I had to forgive why forgiveness is so hard to do for us, but we want it to be so easy for God. It took one day at a time, but I knew it could be done if I continued to pray for them and myself.

Decide not to be trapped in the box alone dealing with this issue like I did and the fear I had with women preachers. I had to learn that forgiveness was not a choice. It had to be done. Jesus said how he could forgive us if we cannot forgive. Then I had fixed my problems from my past. I wanted so much to be accepted that I allowed this pastor to say and do things that in my heart of hearts I knew was not right, that led me to the place I was then in. so I had also to learn to forgive others that had done things to me because I too was holding on the un-forgiveness for things that happen in my youth.

It is hard to love people that hurt and despitefully use you, but we must grow and mature spiritually through the experience and not die spiritually through the experience. One of my main factors of life is now love. I know I was hurt, but I am also committed to helping in the church and being among the people in the church. I know that love does not delight in evil. I had to conclude that I was hurt, and I will be hurt again. We are humans, and humans are not without fault. When hurt happened, I had to learn not to flee but to face the problem head-on, not to bury myself in my box and never to resurface again but to step out on what God has given me, love. We may encounter some hurtful experiences; however, do not let the enemy move you out of fellowship with the institution of the church; (the people of God); because this is not an option for us as believers. We need each other.

Prayer to Overcome Church Hurt Trauma

Father in Jesus' name,
I come before you, with the fact that the church has hurt me. Lord, I am not accepting their behavior, and sometimes it may make it hard for me to trust them again. But God, I do forgive them. I forgive them, Lord, because I love them as you love me. I must be able to forgive so I can be free. So, God, I forgive them for me I let them go God and move on with my life I give them to you, and I give the situation to you because I know you can handle it better than I can, I know holding on to what they have done to me will only hurt me and not them. So, God, thank you for my healing, for my deliverance, and for allowing me to come to the throne with this. Everything Lord, I ask in your son

Jesus name,

amen.

Reminders that Affirm God's Love for YOU!

These things God used people to speak to me; they helped me escape the little black box.

I had first to give myself some affirmations and reminders. I began to love myself for who I was, who I am, who I was to become, and remind myself of to whom I belong. I had to speak life into myself.

- At the beginning of every day, wake up and speak life over yourself.
- Before you lay down at night, speak life over yourself.
- Do NOT be dominated by negativity, internally or externally.

- Be intentional about letting go of burdens that God NEVER called you to bare.
- Uplift yourself and others.
- Learn to love all of you; your body, curves, hair, skin, and everything within.
- Remember that you are more than your circumstances.
- Remember that no one has a heaven or hell to put you in; therefore, no one has the power to tell you how to feel about anything or anybody.
- Remember that you have the power and ability to get everything you desire in life. You are not only innovative but very much capable of achieving greatness.

- Remember, YOU CAN do all things through Christ Jesus who strengthens you! – Philippians 4:13
- Take every day as a new day to start over and do better than the day before.
- Do not compete with anyone but yourself. Remember that God abides in YOU!
- YOU are beautiful, and no man can take that from YOU!
- God created You in his image, and for that reason, all things made and from God are good.
- It is okay to say No. It is a complete sentence. – Pastor Debra Cheek
- Stop giving yourself away to any and everyone.

- Always choose YOU if no one else does not.
- Be productive with every day God has blessed you with on this earth and use it to give him glory.
- Remember that you are the best you can be, and every decision you make may not be good, but you can make better ones every day that you LIVE.
- Remember, there is nothing you cannot have if according to God's will for your life that you cannot have, so go after it with all you have in this life.
- Write down everything you wish to achieve, and do not stop until you have completed them all, especially the one for that day.

- You are resilient and stay that way in all things.
- Happiness is the best path in this world to choose, and you deserve to be happy; do not let anyone steal your joy.
- Remember that Joy comes from the Lord, and only he can give it and take it away.
- Enjoy every second of every moment of your life.
- Do Not ever neglect to pour into yourself.
- You are worth everything you have to offer you.
- If it makes you feel good and God-inspired, then do it!

- Do things you have never done before and do not regret doing it.
- Remember that you deserve to have real love in your life; you deserve to be treated with kindness and respect for everyone you encounter.
- Be God confident and know that it is the key.
- Approach everything challenging and all that happens in your life with zest and gratefulness.
- Stop apologizing for being who God had designed you to be.
- You are allowed to set boundaries in your life, and it is okay to stick to them.
- Remember that when you go through things in this life, it is for you

to learn and grow from it and even for someone else.
- Be grateful that God gave you that privilege to have such a task put in your path.
- Remember, people can and will be mean, but no matter what people say or do to you, you know that you are a loving, caring friend to all you encounter.
- Stay ahead of your feelings; you are in control of them, along with your failures and your successes.
- You do not have to settle for less than the best from anyone, including yourself.
- You are worth all the time you put into yourself and more.

- Know that God had made all that you will ever need, and whatever you lack, he has.
- Stop saying you cannot because you can do all things through Christ Jesus.
- Remember that negative thoughts are here to keep you contained in a place of darkness; always surround yourself with positiveness.
- Do not allow your fears to overcome you; follow God's path before you and overcome the concern.
- Make amends with who you are, your true self, and do it daily.
- You are worthy enough to exist in this world, so make your mark in it while you are here.

- God will always lead you and guide you in the right direction; go and learn.
- Release all the hurt and resentment on your heart, do not hold on to it because it will cause you to die right in your little black box.

NOW, hand over the keys! *The Little Black Box* no longer belongs to you, for God has evicted you, and you are now free to share to others how being in the shadow of death can sometimes lead you to the path of righteousness!!!

BOOK REVIEW

BY TIFFANY ROGERS

"

As I read the book by Ms. McGee, I appreciated her transparency and authenticity. Her willingness to share her traumas from childhood allowed me to gain better insight into her experiences. She often stated her awareness of other people who may have had more intense childhoods. This section encouraged the reader to keep wanting more.

Tiffany Rogers,
LCMHS, LCASA, NCC, CSOTS, CSATS, TF-CBT
Licensed Clinical Mental Health Counselor
Cary, NC

BOOK REVIEW

BY DEBRA CHEEK

❝

Honest. Raw. Challenging. Tonya McGee's new book, "The Little Black Box," brings these words to mind. Her transparent discussion of the challenges she faced and the issues of her soul will provoke all those who read this book to examine their hearts and the contents of their little black box. It will lead you to decide what to keep and what to let go of, and it will inspire the courage to do what is necessary to move forward amid hardship and trials. This book is a beautiful illustration of how our bravery in telling our stories can lead to healing and deliverance for others. If you want freedom, this is the book for you.

Pastor Debra Cheek
Founder of Believing Wives
Durham, NC

BOOK REVIEW

BY ROBIN A. HARRIS

"

This book was just what I needed to help me complete my final steps of forgiveness with my abusers. So much of my personal story paralleled Dr. Mcgee's; I am grateful that a book of such a touchy conversation has been created and given to you by God himself to help others in this awful ordeal. The good news is that God has never left or forsaken you and has proven over and over that he never will. Thank you for sharing your story. I am more than confident that this book will take the world by storm and that God himself will show favor.

Peace and God's Blessings to you in Abundance for your obedience.

Robin A. Harris
Prophetess| Seer| Intercessor
Shekinah Glory Ministries

ABOUT THE AUTHOR

Tonya N. McGee

Is a warrior intercessor and called to healing and deliverance. She began by breaking the curses from over her bloodline.

Dr. Tonya McGee Started this journey in Nov. 1997; though there have been some bumps in the road, she knew that this was the path she needed and wanted to be on. She loves God and everything about what God has called her to be.

Dr. Tonya is the only Daughter of Lucinda McGee and the second oldest of James Mayo. She has three beautiful children Malcolm, Tony, and Destinee. She grew up in NC and decided never to leave. Dr. Tonya wants to encourage people that there is a light on the other side of 'through', no matter what they are going through.

Contact her at:

TonyaMcGeeWrites@gmail.com

Made in the USA
Columbia, SC
01 December 2023